THE UPGRADE AIR FRYER

· Cookbook 2023 ·

1600 Quick, Easy and Yummy Air Fryer Recipes for Everyday Healthy Homemade Meals Incl. Tips and Tricks

Annie Hines

Participate In Recipe Customization!

Record the Meals that Amazing You and Your Family!

CONTENTS

INTRODUCTION 5

Shopping Lists 6

Breakfast & Snacks And Fries Recipes 7

Sauces & Snack And Appetiser Recipes 14

Vegetarian & Vegan Recipes 21

Poultry Recipes 29

Beef & Lamb And Pork Recipes 37

Fish & Seafood Recipes 45

Side Dishes Recipes 53

Desserts Recipes 61

Measurement Conversions 69

Appendix : Recipes Index 73

INTRODUCTION

Greetings, and let's embark on an epicurean odyssey that promises to revolutionize your approach to cooking—the marvelous journey through "Annie Hines's Air Fryer Cookbook." Picture a world where culinary creativity knows no bounds, and the air fryer stands as the gateway to a realm of healthier yet tantalizingly tasty meals. As a devoted home cook and a fervent admirer of the air fryer's prowess, I'm overjoyed to be your guide on this gastronomic expedition. In these carefully crafted pages, we're about to unravel the magic that happens when hot air meets your favorite ingredients, transforming them into crispy, succulent creations that will dazzle your taste buds.

The air fryer, with its ingenious technology, has become my muse in the kitchen. It's a culinary powerhouse that lets you savor the pleasures of fried foods with a fraction of the oil traditionally used. Throughout this cookbook, we'll dive into a plethora of recipes that showcase the air fryer's versatility. From appetizers that have a delightful crunch to entrees that are succulent and perfectly seared, and not to forget desserts that are a sweet revelation—each recipe has been meticulously designed to make the most of this fantastic kitchen tool.

But this cookbook is more than just a collection of recipes; it's an invitation to a lifestyle where convenience, health, and flavor coalesce. It's about celebrating the art of cooking and discovering a world where every dish is an opportunity for creativity and nourishment. Together, we'll debunk the myth that healthy eating has to be bland or time-consuming. With the air fryer by our side, we'll make cooking a joyous adventure, where wholesome meals are effortlessly prepared and indulgence is guilt-free.

So, gear up for an exciting culinary escapade, and let's uncover the possibilities that await within the air fryer's magical chamber. Welcome to a world where taste knows no compromise, and the journey through each recipe is as delightful as the first bite.

Date: ____________________________

MY SHOPPING LIST

Breakfast & Snacks And Fries Recipes

Monte Cristo Breakfast Sandwich 8

Bocconcini Balls 8

Sweet Potato Fries 9

Polenta Fries 9

European Pancakes 10

French Toast 10

Breakfast Sausage Burgers 11

Loaded Hash Browns 11

Courgette Fries 12

Meaty Egg Cups 12

Tangy Breakfast Hash 13

Cheesy Sausage Breakfast Pockets 13

Monte Cristo Breakfast Sandwich

Servings: 4

Cooking Time:xx

Ingredients:

- 1 egg
- 2 slices of sandwich bread
- 1/4 tsp vanilla extract
- 4 slices of sliced Swiss cheese
- 4 slices of sliced deli ham
- 4 slices of sliced turkey
- 1 tsp melted butter
- Powdered sugar for serving

Directions:

1. In a small bowl, mix together the egg and vanilla extract, combining well
2. Take your bread and assemble your sandwich, starting with a slice of cheese, then the ham, turkey, and then another slice of the cheese, with the other slice of bread on the top
3. Compress the sandwich a little, so it cooks better
4. Take a piece of cooking foil and brush over it with the butter
5. Take your sandwich and dip each side into the egg mixture, leaving it to one side for around half a minute
6. Place the sandwich on the foil and place it inside your fryer
7. Cook at 200°C for around 10 minutes, before turning the sandwich over and cooking for another 8 minutes
8. Transfer your sandwich onto a plate and sprinkle with a little powdered sugar

Bocconcini Balls

Servings: 2

Cooking Time:xx

Ingredients:

- 70 g/½ cup plus ½ tablespoon plain/all-purpose flour (gluten-free if you wish)
- 1 egg, beaten
- 70 g/1 cup dried breadcrumbs (gluten-free if you wish; see page 9)
- 10 bocconcini

Directions:

1. Preheat the air-fryer to 200°C/400°F.
2. Place the flour, egg and breadcrumbs on 3 separate plates. Dip each bocconcini ball first in the flour to coat, then the egg, shaking off any excess before rolling in the breadcrumbs.
3. Add the breaded bocconcini to the preheated air-fryer and air-fry for 5 minutes (no need to turn them during cooking). Serve immediately.

Sweet Potato Fries

Servings: 4

Cooking Time:xx

Ingredients:

- 2 medium sweet potatoes
- 2 teaspoons olive oil
- ½ teaspoon salt
- ½ teaspoon chilli/hot red pepper flakes
- ½ teaspoon smoked paprika

Directions:

1. Preheat the air-fryer to 190°C/375°F.
2. Peel the sweet potatoes and slice into fries about 1 x 1 cm/½ x ½ in. by the length of the potato. Toss the sweet potato fries in the oil, salt, chilli and paprika, making sure every fry is coated.
3. Tip into the preheated air-fryer in a single layer (you may need to cook them in two batches, depending on the size of your air-fryer). Air-fry for 10 minutes, turning once halfway during cooking. Serve immediately.

Polenta Fries

Servings: 6

Cooking Time:xx

Ingredients:

- 800 ml/scant 3½ cups water
- 1½ vegetable stock cubes
- ¾ teaspoon dried oregano
- ¾ teaspoon freshly ground black pepper
- 200 g/1⅓ cups quick-cook polenta/cornmeal
- 2 teaspoons olive oil
- 55 g/6 tablespoons plain/all-purpose flour (gluten-free if you wish)
- garlic mayonnaise, to serve

Directions:

1. Bring the water and stock cubes to the boil in a saucepan with the oregano and black pepper. Stir in the polenta/cornmeal and continue to stir until the mixture becomes significantly more solid and is hard to stir – this should take about 5–6 minutes.
2. Grease a 15 x 15-cm/6 x 6-in. baking pan with some of the olive oil. Tip the polenta into the baking pan, smoothing down with the back of a wet spoon. Leave to cool at room temperature for about 30 minutes, then pop into the fridge for at least an hour.
3. Remove the polenta from the fridge and carefully tip out onto a chopping board. Slice the polenta into fingers 7.5 x 1 x 2 cm/3 x ½ x ¾ in. Roll the polenta fingers in the flour, then spray or drizzle the remaining olive oil over the fingers.
4. Preheat the air-fryer to 200°C/400°F.
5. Lay the fingers apart from one another in a single layer in the preheated air-fryer (you may need to cook these in batches, depending on the size of your air-fryer). Air-fry for 9 minutes, turning once halfway through cooking. Serve immediately with garlic mayonnaise.

European Pancakes

Servings: 5

Cooking Time:xx

Ingredients:

- 3 large eggs
- 130g flour
- 140ml whole milk
- 2 tbsp unsweetened apple sauce
- A pinch of salt

Directions:

1. Set your fryer to 200ºC and add five ramekins inside to heat up
2. Place all your ingredients inside a blender to combine
3. Spray the ramekins with a little cooking spray
4. Pour the batter into the ramekins carefully
5. Fry for between 6-8 minutes, depending on your preference
6. Serve with your favourite toppings

French Toast

Servings: 2

Cooking Time:xx

Ingredients:

- 2 beaten eggs
- 2 tbsp softened butter
- 4 slices of sandwich bread
- 1 tsp cinnamon
- 1 tsp nutmeg
- 1 tsp ground cloves
- 1 tsp maple syrup

Directions:

1. Preheat your fryer to 180ºC
2. Take a bowl and add the eggs, salt, cinnamon, nutmeg, and cloves, combining well
3. Take your bread and butter each side, cutting into strips
4. Dip the bread slices into the egg mixture
5. Arrange each slice into the basket of your fryer
6. Cook for 2 minutes
7. Take the basket out and spray with a little cooking spray
8. Turn over the slices and place back into the fryer
9. Cook for 4 minutes
10. Remove and serve with maple syrup

Breakfast Sausage Burgers

Servings: 2

Cooking Time:xx

Ingredients:

- 8 links of your favourite sausage
- Salt and pepper to taste

Directions:

1. Remove the sausage from the skins and use a fork to create a smooth mixture
2. Season to your liking
3. Shape the sausage mixture into burgers or patties
4. Preheat your air fryer to 260ºC
5. Arrange the burgers in the fryer, so they are not touching each other
6. Cook for 8 minutes
7. Serve still warm

Loaded Hash Browns

Servings: 4

Cooking Time:xx

Ingredients:

- 4 large potatoes
- 2 tbsp bicarbonate of soda
- 1 tbsp salt
- 1 tbsp black pepper
- 1 tsp cayenne pepper
- 2 tbsp olive oil
- 1 large chopped onion
- 1 chopped red pepper
- 1 chopped green pepper

Directions:

1. Grate the potatoes
2. Squeeze out any water contained within the potatoes
3. Take a large bowl of water and add the potatoes
4. Add the bicarbonate of soda, combine everything and leave to soak for 25 minutes
5. Drain the water away and carefully pat the potatoes to dry
6. Transfer your potatoes into another bowl
7. Add the spices and oil
8. Combining everything well, tossing to coat evenly
9. Place your potatoes into your fryer basket
10. Set to 200ºC and cook for 10 minutes
11. Give the potatoes a shake and add the peppers and the onions
12. Cook for another 10 minutes

Courgette Fries

Servings: 2

Cooking Time:xx

Ingredients:

- 1 courgette/zucchini
- 3 tablespoons plain/all-purpose flour (gluten-free if you wish)
- ¼ teaspoon salt
- ¼ teaspoon freshly ground black pepper
- 60 g/¾ cup dried breadcrumbs (gluten-free if you wish; see page 9)
- 1 teaspoon dried oregano
- 20 g/¼ cup finely grated Parmesan
- 1 egg, beaten

Directions:

1. Preheat the air-fryer to 180°C/350°F.
2. Slice the courgette/zucchini into fries about 1.5 x 1.5 x 5 cm/⅝ x ⅝ x 2 in.
3. Season the flour with salt and pepper. Combine the breadcrumbs with the oregano and Parmesan.
4. Dip the courgettes/zucchini in the flour (shaking off any excess flour), then the egg, then the seasoned breadcrumbs.
5. Add the fries to the preheated air-fryer and air-fry for 15 minutes. They should be crispy on the outside but soft on the inside. Serve immediately.

Meaty Egg Cups

Servings: 4

Cooking Time:xx

Ingredients:

- 8 slices of toasted sandwich bread
- 2 slices of ham
- 4 eggs
- Salt and pepper to taste
- Butter for greasing

Directions:

1. Take 4 ramekins and grease the insides with a little butter
2. Flatten the slices of toast with a rolling pin and arrange inside the ramekins - two in each
3. Line the inside of each ramekin with a slice of ham
4. Crack one egg into each ramekin
5. Season with a little salt and pepper
6. Place the ramekins into the air fryer and cook at 160°C for 15 minutes
7. Remove from the fryer and wait to cool just slightly
8. Remove and serve

Tangy Breakfast Hash

Servings: 6

Cooking Time:xx

Ingredients:

- 2 tbsp olive oil
- 2 sweet potatoes, cut into cubes
- 1 tbsp smoked paprika
- 1 tsp salt
- 1 tsp black pepper
- 2 slices of bacon, cut into small pieces

Directions:

1. Preheat your air fryer to 200°C
2. Pour the olive oil into a large mixing bowl
3. Add the bacon, seasonings, potatoes and toss to evenly coat
4. Transfer the mixture into the air fryer and cook for 12-16 minutes
5. Stir after 10 minutes and continue to stir periodically for another 5 minutes

Cheesy Sausage Breakfast Pockets

Servings: 2

Cooking Time:xx

Ingredients:

- 1 packet of regular puff pastry
- 4 sausages, cooked and crumbled into pieces
- 5 eggs
- 50g cooked bacon
- 50g grated cheddar cheese

Directions:

1. Scramble your eggs in your usual way
2. Add the sausage and the bacon as you are cooking the eggs and combine well
3. Take your pastry sheets and cut rectangular shapes
4. Add a little of the egg and meat mixture to one half of each pastry piece
5. Fold the rectangles over and use a fork to seal down the edges
6. Place your pockets into your air fryer and cook at 190°C for 10 minutes
7. Allow to cool before serving

Sauces & Snack And Appetiser Recipes

Corn Nuts 15

Thai Bites 15

Pasta Chips 16

Pork Jerky 16

Spicy Chickpeas 17

Air-fried Pickles 17

Salt And Vinegar Chickpeas 18

Roasted Almonds 18

Mac & Cheese Bites 18

Korean Chicken Wings 19

Spicy Peanuts 19

Cheese Wontons 20

Onion Pakoda 20

Corn Nuts

Servings: 8

Cooking Time:xx

Ingredients:

- 1 giant white corn
- 3 tbsp vegetable oil
- 2 tsp salt

Directions:

1. Place the corn in a large bowl, cover with water and sit for 8 hours
2. Drain, pat dry and air dry for 20 minutes
3. Preheat the air fryer to 200ºC
4. Place in a bowl and coat with oil and salt
5. Cook in the air fryer for 10 minutes shake then cook for a further 10 minutes

Thai Bites

Servings: 4

Cooking Time:xx

Ingredients:

- 400g pork mince
- 1 onion
- 1 tsp garlic paste
- 1 tbsp soy
- 1 tbsp Worcester sauce
- Salt and pepper
- 2 tsp Thai curry paste
- ½ lime juice and zest
- 1 tsp mixed spice
- 1 tsp Chinese spice
- 1 tsp coriander

Directions:

1. Place all ingredients in a bowl and mix well
2. Shape into balls
3. Place in the air fryer and cook at 180ºC for 15 minutes

Pasta Chips

Servings: 2

Cooking Time:xx

Ingredients:

- 300g dry pasta bows
- 1 tbsp olive oil
- 1 tbsp nutritional yeast
- 1½ tsp Italian seasoning
- ½ tsp salt

Directions:

1. Cook the pasta for half the time stated on the packet
2. Drain and mix with the oil, yeast, seasoning and salt
3. Place in the air fryer and cook at 200ºC for 5 minutes shake and cook for a further 3 minutes until crunchy

Pork Jerky

Servings: 35

Cooking Time:xx

Ingredients:

- 300g mince pork
- 1 tbsp oil
- 1 tbsp sriracha
- 1 tbsp soy
- ½ tsp pink curing salt
- 1 tbsp rice vinegar
- ½ tsp salt
- ½ tsp pepper
- ½ tsp onion powder

Directions:

1. Mix all ingredients in a bowl until combined
2. Refrigerate for about 8 hours
3. Shape into sticks and place in the air fryer
4. Heat the air fryer to 160ºC
5. Cook for 1 hour turn then cook for another hour
6. Turn again and cook for another hour
7. Cover with paper and sit for 8 hours

Spicy Chickpeas

Servings: 4

Cooking Time:xx

Ingredients:

- 1 can chickpeas
- 1 tbsp yeast
- 1 tbsp olive oil
- 1 tsp paprika
- 1 tsp garlic powder
- ½ tsp salt
- Pinch cumin

Directions:

1. Preheat air fryer to 180ºC
2. Combine all ingredients
3. Add to the air fryer and cook for 22 minutes tossing every 4 minutes until cooked

Air-fried Pickles

Servings: 4

Cooking Time:xx

Ingredients:

- 1/2 cup mayonnaise
- 2 tsp sriracha sauce
- 1 jar dill pickle slices
- 1 egg
- 2 tbsp milk
- 50g flour
- 50g cornmeal
- ½ tsp seasoned salt
- ¼ tsp paprika
- ¼ tsp garlic powder
- ⅛ tsp pepper
- Cooking spray

Directions:

1. Mix the mayo and sriracha together in a bowl and set aside
2. Heat the air fryer to 200ºC
3. Drain the pickles and pat dry
4. Mix egg and milk together, in another bowl mix all the remaining ingredients
5. Dip the pickles in the egg mix then in the flour mix
6. Spray the air fryer with cooking spray
7. Cook for about 4 minutes until crispy

Salt And Vinegar Chickpeas

Servings: 5

Cooking Time:xx

Ingredients:

- 1 can chickpeas
- 100ml white vinegar
- 1 tbsp olive oil
- Salt to taste

Directions:

1. Combine chickpeas and vinegar in a pan, simmer remove from heat and stand for 30 minutes
2. Preheat the air fryer to 190°C
3. Drain chickpeas
4. Place chickpeas in the air fryer and cook for about 4 minutes
5. Pour chickpeas into an ovenproof bowl drizzle with oil, sprinkle with salt
6. Place bowl in the air fryer and cook for another 4 minutes

Roasted Almonds

Servings: 2

Cooking Time:xx

Ingredients:

- 1 tbsp soy sauce
- 1 tbsp garlic powder
- 1 tsp paprika
- ¼ tsp pepper
- 400g raw almonds

Directions:

1. Place all of the ingredients apart from the almonds in a bowl and mix
2. Add the almonds and coat well
3. Place the almonds in the air fryer and cook at 160°C for 6 minutes shaking every 2 minutes

Mac & Cheese Bites

Servings: 14

Cooking Time:xx

Ingredients:

- 200g mac and cheese
- 2 eggs
- 200g panko breadcrumbs
- Cooking spray

Directions:

1. Place drops of mac and cheese on parchment paper and freeze for 1 hour
2. Beat the eggs in a bowl, add the breadcrumbs to another bowl
3. Dip the mac and cheese balls in the egg then into the breadcrumbs
4. Heat the air fryer to 190°C
5. Place in the air fryer, spray with cooking spray and cook for 15 minutes

Korean Chicken Wings

Servings: 2

Cooking Time:xx

Ingredients:

- 25ml soy sauce
- 40g brown sugar
- 2 tbsp hot pepper paste
- 1 tsp sesame oil
- ½ tsp ginger paste
- ½ tsp garlic paste
- 2 green onions, chopped
- 400g chicken wings
- 1 tbsp vegetable oil

Directions:

1. Preheat air fryer to 200ºC
2. Place all ingredients apart from chicken wings and vegetable oil in a pan and simmer for about 4 minutes set aside
3. Massage the vegetable oil into the chicken wings
4. Place in the air fryer and cook for about 10 minutes
5. Turn and cook for a further 10 minutes
6. Coat the wings in the sauce and return to the air fryer
7. Cook for about 2 minutes

Spicy Peanuts

Servings: 8

Cooking Time:xx

Ingredients:

- 2 tbsp olive oil
- 3 tbsp seafood seasoning
- ½ tsp cayenne
- 300g raw peanuts
- Salt to taste

Directions:

1. Preheat the air fryer to 160ºC
2. Whisk together ingredients in a bowl and stir in the peanuts
3. Add to air fryer and cook for 10 minutes, shake then cook for a further 10 minutes
4. Sprinkle with salt and cook for another 5 minutes

Cheese Wontons

Servings: 8

Cooking Time:xx

Ingredients:

- 8 wonton wrappers
- 1 carton pimento cheese
- Small dish of water
- Cooking spray

Directions:

1. Place one tsp of cheese in the middle of each wonton wrapper
2. Brush the edges of each wonton wrapper with water
3. Fold over to create a triangle and seal
4. Heat the air fryer to 190ºC
5. Spray the wontons with cooking spray
6. Place in the air fryer and cook for 3 minutes
7. Turnover and cook for a further 3 minutes

Onion Pakoda

Servings: 2

Cooking Time:xx

Ingredients:

- 200g gram flour
- 2 onions, thinly sliced
- 1 tbsp crushed coriander seeds
- 1 tsp chilli powder
- ¾ tsp salt
- ¼ tsp turmeric
- ¼ tsp baking soda

Directions:

1. Mix all the ingredients together in a large bowl
2. Make bite sized pakodas
3. Heat the air fryer to 200ºC
4. Line the air fryer with foil
5. Place the pakoda in the air fryer and cook for 5 minutes
6. Turn over and cook for a further 5 minutes

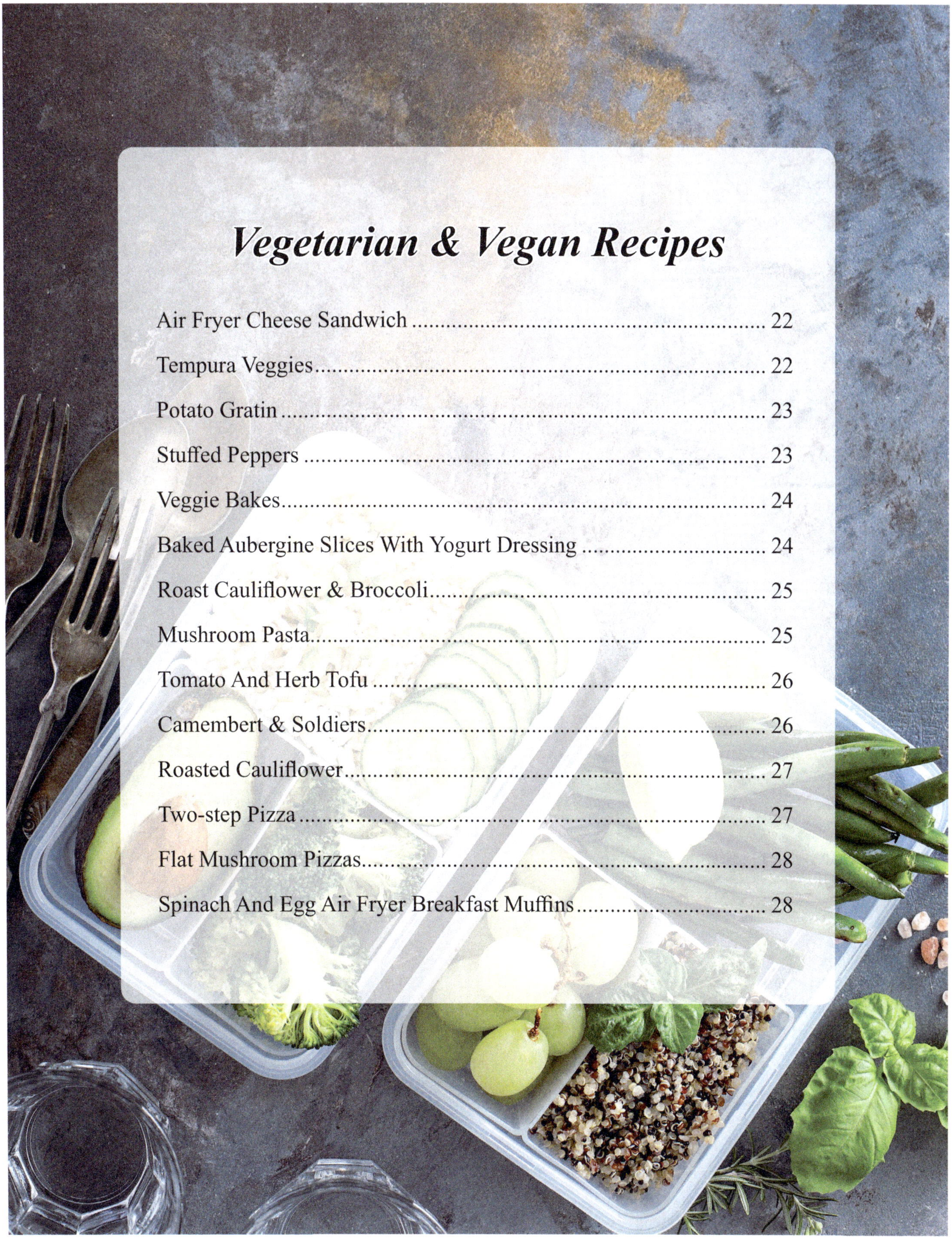

Vegetarian & Vegan Recipes

Air Fryer Cheese Sandwich 22

Tempura Veggies 22

Potato Gratin 23

Stuffed Peppers 23

Veggie Bakes 24

Baked Aubergine Slices With Yogurt Dressing 24

Roast Cauliflower & Broccoli 25

Mushroom Pasta 25

Tomato And Herb Tofu 26

Camembert & Soldiers 26

Roasted Cauliflower 27

Two-step Pizza 27

Flat Mushroom Pizzas 28

Spinach And Egg Air Fryer Breakfast Muffins 28

Air Fryer Cheese Sandwich

Servings:2

Cooking Time:10 Minutes

Ingredients:

- 4 slices white or wholemeal bread
- 2 tbsp butter
- 50 g / 3.5 oz cheddar cheese, grated

Directions:

1. Preheat the air fryer to 180 °C / 350 °F and line the bottom of the basket with parchment paper.
2. Lay the slices of bread out on a clean surface and butter one side of each. Evenly sprinkle the cheese on two of the slices and cover with the final two slices.
3. Transfer the sandwiches to the air fryer, close the lid, and cook for 5 minutes until the bread is crispy and golden, and the cheese is melted.

Tempura Veggies

Servings: 4

Cooking Time:xx

Ingredients:

- 150g flour
- ½ tsp salt
- ½ tsp pepper
- 2 eggs
- 2 tbsp cup water
- 100g avocado wedges
- 100g courgette slices
- 100g panko breadcrumbs
- 2 tsp oil
- 100g green beans
- 100g asparagus spears
- 100g red onion rings
- 100g pepper rings

Directions:

1. Mix together flour, salt and pepper. In another bowl mix eggs and water
2. Stir together panko crumbs and oil in a separate bowl
3. Dip vegetables in the flour mix, then egg and then the bread crumbs
4. Preheat the air fryer to 200°C
5. Place in the air fryer and cook for about 10 minutes until golden brown

Potato Gratin

Servings: 4

Cooking Time:xx

Ingredients:

- 2 large potatoes
- 2 beaten eggs
- 100ml coconut cream
- 1 tbsp plain flour
- 50g grated cheddar

Directions:

1. Slice the potatoes into thin slices, place in the air fryer and cook for 10 minutes at 180ºC
2. Mix eggs, coconut cream and flour together
3. Line four ramekins with the potato slices
4. Cover with the cream mixture, sprinkle with cheese and cook for 10 minutes at 200ºC

Stuffed Peppers

Servings: 6

Cooking Time:xx

Ingredients:

- 250g diced potatoes
- 100g peas
- 1 small onion, diced
- 1 carrot, diced
- 1 bread roll, diced
- 2 garlic cloves, minced
- 2 tsp mixed herbs
- 6 bell peppers
- 100g grated cheese

Directions:

1. Preheat air fryer to 180ºC
2. Combine all the ingredients together apart from the peppers
3. Stuff the peppers with the mix
4. Place in the air fryer and cook for about 20 minutes

Veggie Bakes

Servings: 2

Cooking Time:xx

Ingredients:

- Any type of leftover vegetable bake you have
- 30g flour

Directions:

1. Preheat the air fryer to 180ºC
2. Mix the flour with the leftover vegetable bake
3. Shape into balls and place in the air fryer
4. Cook for 10 minutes

Baked Aubergine Slices With Yogurt Dressing

Servings: 2

Cooking Time:xx

Ingredients:

- 1 aubergine/eggplant, sliced 1.5 cm/⅝ in. thick
- 3 tablespoons olive oil
- ½ teaspoon salt
- YOGURT DRESSING
- 1 small garlic clove
- 1 tablespoon tahini or nut butter
- 100 g/½ cup Greek yogurt
- 2 teaspoons freshly squeezed lemon juice
- 1 tablespoon runny honey
- a pinch of salt
- a pinch of ground cumin
- a pinch of sumac
- TO SERVE
- 30 g/1 oz. rocket/arugula
- 2 tablespoons freshly chopped mint
- 3 tablespoons pomegranate seeds

Directions:

1. Preheat the air-fryer to 180ºC/350ºF.
2. Drizzle the olive oil over each side of the aubergine/eggplant slices. Sprinkle with salt. Add the aubergines to the preheated air-fryer and air-fry for 10 minutes, turning halfway through cooking.
3. Meanwhile, make the dressing by combining all the ingredients in a mini food processor (alterantively, finely chop the garlic, add to a jar with the other ingredients and shake vigorously).
4. Serve the cooked aubergine slices on a bed of rocket/arugula, drizzled with the dressing and with the mint and pomegranate seeds scattered over the top.

Roast Cauliflower & Broccoli

Servings: 6

Cooking Time:xx

Ingredients:

- 300g broccoli
- 300g cauliflower
- 2 tbsp oil
- ½ tsp garlic powder
- ¼ tsp salt
- ¼ tsp paprika
- ⅛ tsp pepper

Directions:

1. Preheat air fryer to 200ºC
2. Place broccoli and cauliflower in a bowl and microwave for 3 minutes
3. Add remaining ingredients and mix well
4. Add to the air fryer and cook for about 12 mins

Mushroom Pasta

Servings: 4

Cooking Time:xx

Ingredients:

- 250g sliced mushrooms
- 1 chopped onion
- 2 tsp minced garlic
- 1 tsp salt
- ½ tsp red pepper flakes
- 75g cup cream
- 70g mascarpone
- 1 tsp dried thyme
- 1 tsp ground black pepper
- ½ cup grated parmesan

Directions:

1. Place all the ingredients in a bowl and mix well
2. Heat the air fryer to 175ºC
3. Grease a 7x3 inch pan and pour in the mixture
4. Place in the air fryer and cook for 15 minutes stirring halfway through
5. Pour over cooked pasta and sprinkle with parmesan

Tomato And Herb Tofu

Servings:4

Cooking Time:10 Minutes

Ingredients:

- 1 x 400 g / 14 oz block firm tofu
- 1 tbsp soy sauce
- 2 tbsp tomato paste
- 1 tsp dried oregano
- 1 tsp dried basil
- 1 tsp garlic powder

Directions:

1. Remove the tofu from the packaging and place on a sheet of kitchen roll. Place another sheet of kitchen roll on top of the tofu and place a plate on top of it.
2. Use something heavy to press the plate down on top of the tofu. Leave for 10 minutes to press the water out of the tofu.
3. Remove the paper towels from the tofu and chop them into even slices that are around ½ cm thick.
4. Preheat the air fryer to 180 °C / 350 °F. Remove the mesh basket from the air fryer machine and line with parchment paper.
5. Place the tofu slices on a lined baking sheet.
6. In a bowl, mix the soy sauce, tomato paste, dried oregano, dried basil, and garlic powder until fully combined.
7. Spread the mixture evenly over the tofu slices. Place the tofu slices on the baking sheet in the lined air fryer basket and cook for 10 minutes until the tofu is firm and crispy.
8. Serve the tofu slices with a side of rice or noodles and some hot vegetables.

Camembert & Soldiers

Servings: 2

Cooking Time:xx

Ingredients:

- 1 piece of Camembert
- 2 slices sandwich bread
- 1 tbsp mustard

Directions:

1. Preheat the air fryer to 180ºC
2. Place the camembert in a sturdy container, cook in the air fryer for 15 minutes
3. Toast the bread and cut into soldiers
4. Serve with the mustard by the side

Roasted Cauliflower

Servings: 2

Cooking Time:xx

Ingredients:

- 3 cloves garlic
- 1 tbsp peanut oil
- ½ tsp salt
- ½ tsp paprika
- 400g cauliflower florets

Directions:

1. Preheat air fryer to 200ºC
2. Crush the garlic, place all ingredients in a bowl and mix well
3. Place in the air fryer and cook for about 15 minutes, shaking every 5 minutes

Two-step Pizza

Servings: 1

Cooking Time:xx

Ingredients:

- BASE
- 130 g/generous ½ cup Greek yogurt
- 125 g self-raising/self-rising flour, plus extra for dusting
- ¼ teaspoon salt
- PIZZA SAUCE
- 100 g/3½ oz. passata/strained tomatoes
- 1 teaspoon dried oregano
- ¼ teaspoon garlic salt
- TOPPINGS
- 75 g/2½ oz. mozzarella, torn
- fresh basil leaves, to garnish

Directions:

1. Mix together the base ingredients in a bowl. Once the mixture starts to look crumbly, use your hands to bring the dough together into a ball. Transfer to a piece of floured parchment paper and roll to about 5 mm/¼ in. thick. Transfer to a second piece of non-floured parchment paper.
2. Preheat the air-fryer to 200ºC/400ºF.
3. Meanwhile, mix the pizza sauce ingredients together in a small bowl and set aside.
4. Prick the pizza base all over with a fork and transfer (on the parchment paper) to the preheated air-fryer and air-fry for 5 minutes. Turn the pizza base over and top with the pizza sauce and the torn mozzarella. Cook for a further 3–4 minutes, until the cheese has melted. Serve immediately with the basil scattered over the top.

Flat Mushroom Pizzas

Servings: 1

Cooking Time:xx

Ingredients:

- 2 portobello mushrooms, cleaned and stalk removed
- 6 mozzarella balls
- 1 teaspoon olive oil
- PIZZA SAUCE
- 100 g/3½ oz. passata/strained tomatoes
- 1 teaspoon dried oregano
- ¼ teaspoon garlic salt

Directions:

1. Preheat the air-fryer to 180ºC/350ºF.
2. Mix the ingredients for the pizza sauce together in a small bowl. Fill each upturned portobello mushroom with sauce, then top each with three mozzarella balls and drizzle the olive oil over.
3. Add the mushrooms to the preheated air-fryer and air-fry for 8 minutes. Serve immediately.

Spinach And Egg Air Fryer Breakfast Muffins

Servings:4

Cooking Time:10 Minutes

Ingredients:

- 8 eggs
- 100 g / 3.5 oz fresh spinach
- 50 g / 1.8 oz cheddar cheese, grated
- ½ onion, finely sliced
- 1 tsp black pepper

Directions:

1. Preheat your air fryer to 200 °C / 400 °F and line an 8-pan muffin tray with parchment paper or grease with olive oil.
2. Gently press the spinach leaves into the bottom of each prepared muffin cup.
3. Sprinkle the finely sliced onion on top of the spinach.
4. Crack 2 eggs into each cup on top of the spinach and add some of the grated cheddar cheese on top of the eggs. Top with a light sprinkle of black pepper.
5. Carefully place the muffins into the air fryer basket and shut the lid. Bake for 10 minutes until the eggs are set and the muffins are hot throughout.
6. Serve the muffins while still hot for breakfast.

Poultry Recipes

Crispy Cornish Hen 30

Turkey Cutlets In Mushroom Sauce 30

Turkey And Mushroom Burgers 31

Buffalo Chicken Wontons 31

Buttermilk Chicken 32

Cheddar & Bbq Stuffed Chicken 32

Spicy Chicken Wing Drummettes 33

Air Fryer Sesame Chicken Thighs 33

Hawaiian Chicken 34

Chicken Kiev 34

Garlic Parmesan Fried Chicken Wings 35

Chicken & Potatoes 35

Bacon Wrapped Chicken Thighs 36

Chicken And Wheat Stir Fry 36

Crispy Cornish Hen

Servings: 4

Cooking Time:xx

Ingredients:

- 2 Cornish hens, weighing around 500g each
- 2 tbsp olive oil
- 1 tsp garlic powder
- 1 tsp paprika
- 1.5 tsp Italian seasoning
- 1 tbsp lemon juice
- Salt and pepper to taste

Directions:

1. Preheat your air fryer to 260ºC
2. Combine all the ingredients into a bowl (except for the hens) until smooth
3. Brush the hens with the mixture, coating evenly
4. Place in the air fryer basket, with the breast side facing down
5. Cook for 35 minutes
6. Turn over and cook for another 10 minutes
7. Ensure the hens are white in the middle before serving

Turkey Cutlets In Mushroom Sauce

Servings: 2

Cooking Time:xx

Ingredients:

- 2 turkey cutlets
- 1 tbsp butter
- 1 can of cream of mushroom sauce
- 160ml milk
- Salt and pepper for seasoning

Directions:

1. Preheat the air fryer to 220ºC
2. Brush the turkey cults with the butter and seasoning
3. Place in the air fryer and cook for 11 minutes
4. Add the mushroom soup and milk to a pan and cook over the stone for around 10 minutes, stirring every so often
5. Top the turkey cutlets with the sauce

Turkey And Mushroom Burgers

Servings: 2

Cooking Time:xx

Ingredients:

- 180g mushrooms
- 500g minced turkey
- 1 tbsp of your favourite chicken seasoning, e.g. Maggi
- 1 tsp onion powder
- 1 tsp garlic powder
- Salt and pepper to taste

Directions:

1. Place the mushrooms in a food processor and puree
2. Add all the seasonings and mix well
3. Remove from the food processor and transfer to a mixing bowl
4. Add the minced turkey and combine again
5. Shape the mix into 5 burger patties
6. Spray with cooking spray and place in the air fryer
7. Cook at 160ºC for 10 minutes, until cooked.

Buffalo Chicken Wontons

Servings: 6

Cooking Time:xx

Ingredients:

- 200g shredded chicken
- 1 tbsp buffalo sauce
- 4 tbsp softened cream cheese
- 1 sliced spring onion
- 2 tbsp blue cheese crumbles
- 12 wonton wrappers

Directions:

1. Preheat the air fryer to 200ºC
2. Take a bowl and combine the chicken and buffalo sauce
3. In another bowl mix the cream cheese until a smooth consistency has formed and then combine the scallion blue cheese and seasoned chicken
4. Take the wonton wrappers and run wet fingers along each edge
5. Place 1 tbsp of the filling into the centre of the wonton and fold the corners together
6. Cook at 200ºC for 3 to 5 minutes, until golden brown

Buttermilk Chicken

Servings: 4

Cooking Time:xx

Ingredients:

- 500g chicken thighs, skinless and boneless
- 180ml buttermilk
- 40g tapioca flour
- ½ tsp garlic salt
- 1 egg
- 75g all purpose flour
- ½ tsp brown sugar
- 1 tsp garlic powder
- ½ tsp paprika
- ½ tsp onion powder
- ¼ tsp oregano
- Salt and pepper to taste

Directions:

1. Take a medium mixing bowl and combine the buttermilk and hot sauce
2. Add the tapioca flour, garlic salt and black pepper in a plastic bag and shake
3. Beat the egg
4. Take the chicken thighs and tip into the buttermilk, then the tapioca mixture, the egg, and then the flour
5. Preheat air fryer to 190°C
6. Cook the chicken thighs for 10 minutes, until white in the middle

Cheddar & Bbq Stuffed Chicken

Servings: 2

Cooking Time:xx

Ingredients:

- 3 strips of bacon
- 100g cheddar cheese
- 3 tbsp barbecue sauce
- 300g skinless and boneless chicken breasts
- salt and ground pepper to taste

Directions:

1. Preheat the air fryer to 190°C
2. Cook one of the back strips for 2 minutes, before cutting into small pieces
3. Increase the temperature of the air fryer to 200°C
4. Mix together the cooked bacon, cheddar cheese and 1 tbsp barbecue sauce
5. Take the chicken and make a pouch by cutting a 1 inch gap into the top
6. Stuff the pouch with the bacon and cheese mixture and then wrap around the chicken breast
7. Coat the chicken with the rest of the BBQ sauce
8. Cook for 10 minutes in the air fryer, before turning and cooking for an additional 10 minutes

Spicy Chicken Wing Drummettes

Servings: 4

Cooking Time:xx

Ingredients:

- 10 large chicken drumettes
- Cooking spray
- 100ml rice vinegar
- 3 tbsp honey
- 2 tbsp unsalted chicken stock
- 1 tbsp lower sodium soy sauce
- 1 tbsp toasted sesame oil
- ⅜ tsp crushed red pepper
- 1 garlic clove, finely chopped
- 2 tbsp chopped, unsalted, roasted peanuts
- 1 tbsp chopped fresh chives

Directions:

1. Coat the chicken in cooking spray and place inside the air fryer
2. Cook at 200ºC for 30 minutes
3. Take a mixing bowl and combine the vinegar, honey, stock, soy sauce, oil, crushed red pepper and garlic
4. Cook to a simmer, until a syrup consistency is achieved
5. Coat the chicken in this mixture and sprinkle with peanuts and chives

Air Fryer Sesame Chicken Thighs

Servings: 4

Cooking Time:xx

Ingredients:

- 2 tbsp sesame oil
- 2 tbsp soy sauce
- 1 tbsp honey
- 1 tbsp sriracha sauce
- 1 tsp rice vinegar
- 400g chicken thighs
- 1 green onion, chopped
- 2 tbsp toasted sesame seeds

Directions:

1. Take a large bowl and combine the sesame oil, soy sauce, honey, sriracha and vinegar
2. Add the chicken and refrigerate for 30 minutes
3. Preheat the air fryer to 200ºC
4. Cook for 5 minutes
5. Flip and then cook for another 10 minutes
6. Serve with green onion and sesame seeds

Hawaiian Chicken

Servings: 2

Cooking Time:xx

Ingredients:

- 2 chicken breasts
- 1 tbsp butter
- A pinch of salt and pepper
- 160ml pineapple juice
- 25g brown sugar
- 3 tbsp soy sauce
- 2 tsp water
- 1 clove of garlic, minced
- 1 tsp grated ginger
- 2 tsp cornstarch

Directions:

1. Preheat the air fryer to 260ºC
2. Take a bowl and combine the butter and salt and pepper
3. Cover the chicken with the butter and cook in the fryer for 15 minutes, turning halfway
4. Remove and allow to rest for 5 minutes
5. Take another bowl and mix together the pineapple juice, soy sauce, garlic, ginger, and brown sugar
6. Transfer to a saucepan and simmer for 5 minutes
7. Combine the water and cornstarch and add to the sauce, stirring continually for another minute
8. Slice the chicken into strips and pour the sauce over the top

Chicken Kiev

Servings: 4

Cooking Time:xx

Ingredients:

- 4 boneless chicken breasts
- 4 tablespoons plain/all-purpose flour (gluten-free if you wish)
- 1 egg, beaten
- 130 g/2 cups dried breadcrumbs (gluten-free if you wish, see page 9)
- GARLIC BUTTER
- 60 g/4 tablespoons salted butter, softened
- 1 large garlic clove, finely chopped

Directions:

1. Mash together the butter and garlic. Form into a sausage shape, then slice into 4 equal discs. Place in the freezer until frozen.
2. Make a deep horizontal slit across each chicken breast, taking care not to cut through to the other side. Stuff the cavity with a disc of frozen garlic butter. Place the flour in a shallow bowl, the egg in another and the breadcrumbs in a third. Coat each chicken breast first in flour, then egg, then breadcrumbs.
3. Preheat the air-fryer to 180ºC/350ºF.
4. Add the chicken Kievs to the preheated air-fryer and air-fry for 12 minutes until cooked through. This is hard to gauge as the butter inside the breast is not an indicator of doneness, so test the meat in the centre with a meat thermometer – it should be at least 75ºC/167ºF; if not, cook for another few minutes.

Garlic Parmesan Fried Chicken Wings

Servings: 4

Cooking Time:xx

Ingredients:

- 16 chicken wing drumettes
- Cooking spray
- 240ml low fat buttermilk
- 150g flour
- 140g grated parmesan
- 2 tbsp low sodium soy sauce
- 1 sachet of your favourite chicken seasoning
- 1 tsp garlic powder
- Salt and pepper to taste

Directions:

1. Place the chicken onto a cooking tray and pour the soy sauce over the top, ensuring it is fully coated
2. Season the chicken and place in the refrigerator for 30 minutes
3. Add the flour and parmesan into a ziplock bag
4. Coat the chicken with buttermilk and add it to the ziplock bag with the flour
5. Preheat your air fryer to 200ºC
6. Place the chicken into the air fryer for 20 minutes
7. Shake the air fryer basket every 5 minutes until the 20 minutes is up

Chicken & Potatoes

Servings: 4

Cooking Time:xx

Ingredients:

- 2 tbsp olive oil
- 2 potatoes, cut into 2" pieces
- 2 chicken breasts, cut into pieces of around 1" size
- 4 crushed garlic cloves
- 2 tsp smoked paprika
- 1 tsp thyme
- 1/2 tsp red chilli flakes
- Salt and pepper to taste

Directions:

1. Preheat your air fryer to 260ºC
2. Take a large bowl and combine the potatoes with half of the garlic, half the paprika, half the chilli flakes, salt, pepper and half the oil
3. Place into the air fryer and cook for 5 minutes, before turning over and cooking for another 5 minutes
4. Take a bowl and add the chicken with the rest of the seasonings and oil, until totally coated
5. Add the chicken to the potatoes mixture, moving the potatoes to the side
6. Cook for 10 minutes, turning the chicken halfway through

Bacon Wrapped Chicken Thighs

Servings: 4

Cooking Time:xx

Ingredients:

- 75g softened butter
- ½ clove minced garlic
- ¼ tsp dried thyme
- ¼ tsp dried basil
- ⅛ tsp coarse salt
- 100g thick cut bacon
- 350g chicken thighs, boneless and skinless
- 2 tsp minced garlic
- Salt and pepper to taste

Directions:

1. Take a mixing bowl and add the softened butter, garlic, thyme, basil, salt and pepper, combining well
2. Place the butter onto a sheet of plastic wrap and roll up to make a butter log
3. Refrigerate for about 2 hours
4. Remove the plastic wrap
5. Place one bacon strip onto the butter and then place the chicken thighs on top of the bacon. Sprinkle with garlic
6. Place the cold butter into the middle of the chicken thigh and tuck one end of bacon into the chicken
7. Next, fold over the chicken thigh whilst rolling the bacon around
8. Repeat with the rest
9. Preheat the air fryer to 188C
10. Cook the chicken until white in the centre and the juices run clear

Chicken And Wheat Stir Fry

Servings: 4

Cooking Time:xx

Ingredients:

- 1 onion
- 1 clove of garlic
- 200g skinless boneless chicken breast halves
- 3 whole tomatoes
- 400ml water
- 1 chicken stock cube
- 1 tbsp curry powder
- 130g wheat berries
- 1 tbsp vegetable oil

Directions:

1. Thinly slice the onion and garlic
2. Chop the chicken and tomatoes into cubes
3. Take a large saucepan and add the water, chicken stock, curry powder and wheat berries, combining well
4. Pour the oil into the air fryer bowl and heat for 5 minutes at 200ºC
5. Add the remaining ingredients and pour the contents into the air fryer
6. Cook for 15 minutes

Beef & Lamb And Pork Recipes

Buttermilk Pork Chops 38
Pork Chilli Cheese Dogs 38
Lamb Burgers 39
Homemade Crispy Pepperoni Pizza 39
Salt And Pepper Belly Pork 40
Vegetable & Beef Frittata 40
Traditional Empanadas 41
Jamaican Jerk Pork 41
Steak Dinner 42
Pork Taquitos 42
Pork Chops With Raspberry And Balsamic 43
Tahini Beef Bites 43
Butter Steak & Asparagus 44
Beef Satay 44

Beef & Lamb And Pork Recipes

Buttermilk Pork Chops

Servings: 4

Cooking Time:xx

Ingredients:

- 4 pork chops
- 3 tbsp buttermilk
- 75g flour
- Cooking oil spray
- 1 packet of pork rub
- Salt and pepper to taste

Directions:

1. Rub the chops with the pork rub
2. Place the pork chops in a bowl and drizzle with buttermilk
3. Coat the chops with flour
4. Place in the air fryer and cook at 190°C for 15 minutes turning halfway

Pork Chilli Cheese Dogs

Servings: 2

Cooking Time:xx

Ingredients:

- 1 can of pork chilli, or chilli you have left over
- 200g grated cheese
- 2 hot dog bread rolls
- 2 hot dogs

Directions:

1. Preheat the air fryer to 260°C
2. Cook the hot dogs for 4 minutes, turning halfway
3. Place the hotdogs inside the bread rolls and place back inside the air fryer
4. Top with half the cheese on top and then the chilli
5. Add the rest of the cheese
6. Cook for an extra 2 minutes

Lamb Burgers

Servings: 4

Cooking Time:xx

Ingredients:

- 600g minced lamb
- 2 tsp garlic puree
- 1 tsp harissa paste
- 2 tbsp Moroccan spice
- Salt and pepper

Directions:

1. Place all the ingredients in a bowl and mix well
2. Form into patties
3. Place in the air fryer and cook at 180ºC for 18 minutes

Homemade Crispy Pepperoni Pizza

Servings:4

Cooking Time:10 Minutes

Ingredients:

- For the pizza dough:
- 500 g / 17.6 oz plain flour
- 1 tsp salt
- 1 tsp dry non-fast-acting yeast
- 400 ml warm water
- For the toppings:
- 100 g / 3.5 oz tomato sauce
- 100 g / 3.5 oz mozzarella cheese, grated
- 8 slices pepperoni

Directions:

1. To make the pizza dough, place the plain flour, salt, and dry yeast in a large mixing bowl. Pour in the warm water bit by bit until it forms a tacky dough.
2. Lightly dust a clean kitchen top surface with plain flour and roll the dough out until it is around ½ an inch thick.
3. Preheat your air fryer to 150 °C / 300 °F and line the bottom of the basket with parchment paper.
4. Spread the tomato sauce evenly across the dough and top with grated mozzarella cheese. Top with the pepperoni slices and carefully transfer the pizza into the lined air fryer basket.
5. Cook the pizza until the crust is golden and crispy, and the mozzarella cheese has melted.
6. Enjoy the pizza while still hot with a side salad and some potato wedges.

Salt And Pepper Belly Pork

Servings: 4

Cooking Time:xx

Ingredients:

- 500g belly pork
- 1 tsp pepper
- ½ tsp salt

Directions:

1. Cut the pork into bite size pieces and season with salt and pepper
2. Heat the air fryer to 200ºC
3. Place in the air fryer and cook for 15 minutes until crisp

Vegetable & Beef Frittata

Servings: 2

Cooking Time:xx

Ingredients:

- 250g ground beef
- 4 shredded hash browns
- 8 eggs
- Half a diced onion
- 1 courgette, diced
- 250g grated cheese
- Salt and pepper for seasoning

Directions:

1. Break the ground beef up and place in the air fryer
2. Add the onion and combine well
3. Cook at 260ºC for 3 minutes
4. Stir the mixture and cook foremother 2 minutes
5. Remove and clean the tray
6. Add the courgette to the air fryer and spray with a little cooking oil
7. Cook for 3 minutes
8. Add to the meat mixture and combine
9. Take a mixing bowl and combine the cheese, has browns, and eggs
10. Add the meat and courgette to the bowl and season with salt and pepper
11. Take a 6" round baking tray and add the mixture
12. Cook for 8 minutes before cutting lines in the top and cooking for another 8 minutes
13. Cut into slices before serving

Traditional Empanadas

Servings: 2

Cooking Time:xx

Ingredients:

- 300g minced beef
- 1 tbsp olive oil
- ¼ cup finely chopped onion
- 150g chopped mushrooms
- ⅛ tsp cinnamon
- 4 chopped tomatoes
- 2 tsp chopped garlic
- 6 green olives
- ¼ tsp paprika
- ¼ tsp cumin
- 8 goyoza wrappers
- 1 beaten egg

Directions:

1. Heat oil in a pan add onion and minced beef and cook until browned
2. Add mushrooms and cook for 6 minutes
3. Add garlic, olives, paprika, cumin and cinnamon, and cook for about 3 minutes
4. Stir in tomatoes and cook for 1 minute, set aside allow to cool
5. Place 1 ½ tbsp of filling in each goyoza wrapper
6. Brush edges with egg fold over and seal pinching edges
7. Place in the air fryer and cook at 200 for about 7 minutes

Jamaican Jerk Pork

Servings: 4

Cooking Time:xx

Ingredients:

- 400g pork butt cut into 3 pieces
- 100g jerk paste

Directions:

1. Rub the pork with jerk paste and marinate for 4 hours
2. Preheat air fryer to 190ºC
3. Place pork in the air fryer and cook for about 20 minutes turning halfway

Steak Dinner

Servings: 5

Cooking Time:xx

Ingredients:

- 400g sirloin steak, cut into cubes
- 300g red potatoes, cubed
- 1 pepper
- 1 tsp dried parsley
- ½ tsp pepper
- 2 tsp olive oil
- 1 sliced onion
- 300g chopped mushrooms
- 2 tsp garlic salt
- 2 tsp salt
- 5 tsp butter

Directions:

1. Preheat the air fryer to 200°C
2. Take 5 pieces of foil, layer meat onion, potatoes, mushrooms and pepper in each one
3. Add 1 tsp of butter to each one
4. Mix seasonings and sprinkle over the top
5. Fold the foil and cook for 25-30 minutes

Pork Taquitos

Servings: 5

Cooking Time:xx

Ingredients:

- 400g shredded pork
- 500g grated mozzarella
- 10 flour tortillas
- The juice of 1 lime
- Cooking spray

Directions:

1. Preheat air fryer to 190°C
2. Sprinkle lime juice on the pork and mix
3. Microwave tortilla for about 10 seconds to soften
4. Add a little pork and cheese to a tortilla
5. Roll then tortilla up, and place in the air fryer
6. Cook for about 7 minutes until golden, turn halfway through cooking

Pork Chops With Raspberry And Balsamic

Servings: 4

Cooking Time:xx

Ingredients:

- 2 large eggs
- 30ml milk
- 250g panko bread crumbs
- 250g finely chopped pecans
- 1 tbsp orange juice
- 4 pork chops
- 30ml balsamic vinegar
- 2 tbsp brown sugar
- 2 tbsp raspberry jam

Directions:

1. Preheat air fryer to 200°C
2. Mix the eggs and milk together in a bowl
3. In another bowl mix the breadcrumbs and pecans
4. Coat the pork chops in flour, egg and then coat in the breadcrumbs
5. Place in the air fryer and cook for 12 minutes until golden turning halfway
6. Put the remaining ingredients in a pan simmer for about 6 minutes, serve with the pork chops

Tahini Beef Bites

Servings: 2

Cooking Time:xx

Ingredients:

- 500g sirloin steak, cut into cubes
- 2 tbsp Za'atar seasoning
- 1 tsp olive oil
- 25g Tahini
- 25g warm water
- 1 tbsp lemon juice
- 1 clove of garlic
- Salt to taste

Directions:

1. Preheat the air fryer to 250°C
2. Take a bowl and combine the oil with the steak, salt, and Za'atar seasoning
3. Place in the air fryer and cook for 10 minutes, turning halfway through
4. Take a bowl and combine the water, garlic, lemon juice, salt, and tahini, or use a food processor if you have one

Butter Steak & Asparagus

Servings: 6

Cooking Time:xx

Ingredients:

- 500g steak, cut into 6 pieces
- Salt and pepper
- 75g tamari sauce
- 2 cloves crushed garlic
- 400g asparagus
- 3 sliced peppers
- 25g balsamic vinegar
- 50g beef broth
- 2 tbsp butter

Directions:

1. Season steaks with salt and pepper
2. Place steaks in a bowl, add tamari sauce and garlic make sure steaks are covered, leave to marinate for at least 1hr
3. Place steaks on a board, fill with peppers and asparagus, roll the steak around and secure with tooth picks
4. Set your fryer to 200°C and cook for 5 minutes.
5. Whilst cooking heat the broth, butter and balsamic vinegar in a saucepan until thickened
6. Pour over the steaks and serve

5\. Pour the sauce over the bites and serve

Beef Satay

Servings: 2

Cooking Time:xx

Ingredients:

- 400g steak strips
- 2 tbsp oil
- 1 tbsp fish sauce
- 1 tsp sriracha sauce
- 200g sliced coriander (fresh)
- 1 tsp ground coriander
- 1 tbsp soy
- 1 tbsp minced ginger
- 1 tbsp minced garlic
- 1 tbsp sugar
- 25g roasted peanuts

Directions:

1. Add oil, dish sauce, soy, ginger, garlic, sugar sriracha, coriander and ¼ cup coriander to a bowl and mix. Add the steak and marinate for 30 minutes
2. Add the steak to the air fryer and cook at 200°C for about 8 minutes
3. Place the steak on a plate and top with remaining coriander and chopped peanuts
4. Serve with peanut sauce

Fish & Seafood Recipes

Crunchy Fish 46

Shrimp With Yum Yum Sauce 46

Thai Fish Cakes 47

Peppery Lemon Shrimp 47

Salt & Pepper Calamari 48

Beer Battered Fish Tacos 48

Chilli Lime Tilapia 49

Baked Panko Cod 49

Air Fryer Tuna 50

Lobster Tails 50

Traditional Fish And Chips 50

Ranch Style Fish Fillets 51

Thai Salmon Patties 51

Fish In Foil 51

Traditional Fish And Chips 52

Fish Sticks With Tartar Sauce Batter 52

Fish & Seafood Recipes

Crunchy Fish

Servings: 4

Cooking Time:xx

Ingredients:

- 200g dry breadcrumbs
- 4 tbsp olive oil
- 4 fillets of white fish
- 1 beaten egg
- 1 sliced lemon

Directions:

1. Heat the fryer to 180ºC
2. In a medium mixing bowl, combine the olive oil and the breadcrumbs
3. Take the fish and first dip it into the egg and then the breadcrumbs, making sure they are evenly coated well
4. Arrange the fish into the basket
5. Cook for 12 minutes
6. Remove and serve with lemon slices

Shrimp With Yum Yum Sauce

Servings: 4

Cooking Time:xx

Ingredients:

- 400g peeled jumbo shrimp
- 1 tbsp soy sauce
- 1 tbsp garlic paste
- 1 tbsp ginger paste
- 4 tbsp mayo
- 2 tbsp ketchup
- 1 tbsp sugar
- 1 tsp paprika
- 1 tsp garlic powder

Directions:

1. Mix soy sauce, garlic paste and ginger paste in a bowl. Add the shrimp, allow to marinate for 15 minutes
2. In another bowl mix ketchup, mayo, sugar, paprika and the garlic powder to make the yum yum sauce.
3. Set the air fryer to 200ºC, place shrimp in the basket and cook for 8-10 minutes

Thai Fish Cakes

Servings: 4

Cooking Time:xx

Ingredients:

- 200g pre-mashed potatoes
- 2 fillets of white fish, flaked and mashed
- 1 onion
- 1 tsp butter
- 1 tsp milk
- 1 lime zest and rind
- 3 tsp chilli
- 1 tsp Worcester sauce
- 1 tsp coriander
- 1 tsp mixed spice
- 1 tsp mixed herbs
- 50g breadcrumbs
- Salt and pepper to taste

Directions:

1. Cover the white fish in milk
2. in a mixing bowl place the fish and add the seasoning and mashed potatoes
3. Add the butter and remaining milk
4. Use your hands to create patties and place in the refrigerator for 3 hours
5. Preheat your air fryer to 200°C
6. Cook for 15 minutes

Peppery Lemon Shrimp

Servings: 2

Cooking Time:xx

Ingredients:

- 300g uncooked shrimp
- 1 tbsp olive oil
- 1 the juice of 1 lemon
- 0.25 tsp garlic powder
- 1 sliced lemon
- 1 tsp pepper
- 0.25 tsp paprika

Directions:

1. Heat the fryer to 200°C
2. Take a medium sized mixing bowl and combine the lemon juice, pepper, garlic powder, paprika and the olive oil together
3. Add the shrimp to the bowl and make sure they're well coated
4. Arrange the shrimp into the basket of the fryer
5. Cook for between 6-8 minutes, until firm and pink

Salt & Pepper Calamari

Servings: 2

Cooking Time:xx

Ingredients:

- 500g squid rings
- 500g panko breadcrumbs
- 250g plain flour
- 2 tbsp pepper
- 2 tbsp salt
- 200ml buttermilk
- 1 egg

Directions:

1. Take a medium bowl and combine the buttermilk and egg, stirring well
2. Take another bowl and combine the salt, pepper, flour, and panko breadcrumbs, combining again
3. Dip the quid into the buttermilk first and then the breadcrumbs, coating evenly
4. Place in the air fryer basket
5. Cook at 150ºC for 12 minutes, until golden

Beer Battered Fish Tacos

Servings: 2

Cooking Time:xx

Ingredients:

- 300g cod fillets
- 2 eggs
- 1 can of Mexican beer
- 300g cornstarch
- 300g flour
- 2 soft corn tortillas
- ½ tsp chilli powder
- 1 tbsp cumin
- Salt and pepper to taste

Directions:

1. Whisk together the eggs and beer
2. In a separate bowl whisk together cornstarch, chilli powder, flour, cumin and salt and pepper
3. Coat the fish in the egg mixture then coat in flour mixture
4. Spray the air fryer with non stick spray and add the fish
5. Set your fryer to 170ºC and cook for 15 minutes
6. Place the fish in a corn tortilla

Chilli Lime Tilapia

Servings: 3

Cooking Time:xx

Ingredients:

- 500g Tilapia fillets
- 25g panko crumbs
- 200g flour
- Salt and pepper to taste
- 2 eggs
- 1 tbsp chilli powder
- The juice of 1 lime

Directions:

1. Mix panko, salt and pepper and chilli powder together
2. Whisk the egg in a separate bowl
3. Spray the air fryer with cooking spray
4. Dip the tilapia in the flour, then in the egg and cover in the panko mix
5. Place fish in the air fryer, spray with cooking spray and cook for 7-8 minutes at 190ºC
6. Turn the fish over and cook for a further 7-8 minutes until golden brown.
7. Squeeze lime juice over the top and serve

Baked Panko Cod

Servings: 5

Cooking Time:xx

Ingredients:

- 400g cod, cut into 5 pieces
- 250g panko breadcrumbs
- 1 egg plus 1 egg white extra
- Cooking spray
- ½ tsp onion powder
- ½ tsp garlic salt
- ⅛ tsp black pepper
- ½ tsp mixed herbs

Directions:

1. Heat air fryer to 220ºC
2. Beat the egg and egg white in a bowl
3. Sprinkle fish with herbs and spice mix, dip into the egg and then cover in the panko bread crumbs
4. Line air fryer basket with tin foil. Place the fish in the air fryer and coat with cooking spray
5. Cook for about 15 minutes until, fish is lightly browned

Air Fryer Tuna

Servings: 2

Cooking Time:xx

Ingredients:

- 2 tuna steaks, boneless and skinless
- 2 tsp honey
- 1 tsp grated ginger
- 4 tbsp soy sauce
- 1 tsp sesame oil
- 1/2 tsp rice vinegar

Directions:

1. Combine the honey, soy sauce, rice vinegar and sesame oil in a bowl until totally mixed together
2. Cover the tuna steaks with the sauce and place in the refrigerator for half an hour to marinade
3. Preheat the air fryer to 270ºC
4. Cook the tuna for 4 minutes
5. Allow to rest before slicing

Lobster Tails

Servings: 2

Cooking Time:xx

Ingredients:

- 4 lobster tails
- 2 tbsp melted butter
- ½ tsp salt
- 1 tsp pepper

Directions:

1. Cut the lobster tails through the tail section and pull back the shell
2. Brush with the melted butter and sprinkle with salt and pepper
3. Heat the air fryer to 200ºC and cook for 4 minutes
4. Brush with melted butter and cook for a further 2 minutes

Traditional Fish And Chips

Servings: 4

Cooking Time:xx

Ingredients:

- 4 potatoes, peeled and cut into chips
- 2 fish fillets of your choice
- 1 beaten egg
- 3 slices of wholemeal bread, grated into breadcrumbs
- 25g tortilla crisps
- 1 lemon rind and juice
- 1 tbsp parsley
- Salt and pepper to taste

Directions:

1. Preheat your air fryer to 200ºC
2. Place the chips inside and cook until crispy
3. Cut the fish fillets into 4 slices and season with lemon juice
4. Place the breadcrumbs, lemon rind, parsley, tortillas and seasoning into a food processor and blitz to create a crumb consistency
5. Place the breadcrumbs on a large plate
6. Coat the fish in the egg and then the breadcrumb mixture
7. Cook for 15 minutes at 180ºC

Ranch Style Fish Fillets

Servings: 4

Cooking Time:xx

Ingredients:

- 200g bread crumbs
- 30g ranch-style dressing mix
- 2 tbsp oil
- 2 beaten eggs
- 4 fish fillets of your choice
- Lemon wedges to garnish

Directions:

1. Preheat air fryer to 180ºC
2. Mix the bread crumbs and ranch dressing mix together, add in the oil until the mix becomes crumbly
3. Dip the fish into the, then cover in the breadcrumb mix
4. Place in the air fryer and cook for 12-13 minutes

Thai Salmon Patties

Servings: 7

Cooking Time:xx

Ingredients:

- 1 large can of salmon, drained and bones removed
- 30g panko breadcrumbs
- ¼ tsp salt
- 1 ½ tbsp Thai red curry paste
- 1 ½ tbsp brown sugar
- Zest of 1 lime
- 2 eggs
- Cooking spray

Directions:

1. Take a large bowl and combine all ingredients together until smooth
2. Use your hands to create patties that are around 1 inch in thickness
3. Preheat your air fryer to 180ºC
4. Coat the patties with cooking spray
5. Cook for 4 minutes each side

Fish In Foil

Servings: 2

Cooking Time:xx

Ingredients:

- 1 tablespoon avocado oil or olive oil, plus extra for greasing
- 1 tablespoon soy sauce (or tamari)
- 1½ teaspoons freshly grated garlic
- 1½ teaspoons freshly grated ginger
- 1 small red chilli/chile, finely chopped
- 2 skinless, boneless white fish fillets (about 350 g/12 oz. total weight)

Directions:

1. Mix the oil, soy sauce, garlic, ginger and chilli/chile together. Brush a little oil onto two pieces of foil, then lay the fish in the centre of the foil. Spoon the topping mixture over the fish. Wrap the foil around the fish to make a parcel, with a gap above the fish but shallow enough to fit in your air-fryer basket.
2. Preheat the air-fryer to 180ºC/350ºF.
3. Add the foil parcels to the preheated air-fryer and air-fry for 7–10 minutes, depending on the thickness of your fillets. The fish should just flake when a fork is inserted. Serve immediately.

Traditional Fish And Chips

Servings: 4

Cooking Time:xx

Ingredients:

- 4 potatoes, peeled and cut into chips
- 2 fish fillets of your choice
- 1 beaten egg
- 3 slices of wholemeal bread, grated into breadcrumbs
- 25g tortilla crisps
- 1 lemon rind and juice
- 1 tbsp parsley
- Salt and pepper to taste

Directions:

1. Preheat your air fryer to 200ºC
2. Place the chips inside and cook until crispy
3. Cut the fish fillets into 4 slices and season with lemon juice
4. Place the breadcrumbs, lemon rind, parsley, tortillas and seasoning into a food processor and blitz to create a crumb consistency
5. Place the breadcrumbs on a large plate
6. Coat the fish in the egg and then the breadcrumb mixture
7. Cook for 15 minutes at 180ºC

Fish Sticks With Tartar Sauce Batter

Servings: 4

Cooking Time:xx

Ingredients:

- 6 tbsp mayonnaise
- 2 tbsp dill pickle
- 1 tsp seafood seasoning
- 400g cod fillets, cut into sticks
- 300g panko breadcrumbs

Directions:

1. Combine the mayonnaise, seafood seasoning and dill pickle in a large bowl.
2. Add the cod sticks and coat well
3. Preheat air fryer to 200ºC
4. Coat the fish sticks in the breadcrumbs
5. Place in the air fryer and cook for 12 minutes

Side Dishes Recipes

Sweet Potato Wedges 54

Sweet Potato Tots 54

Ranch-style Potatoes 55

Homemade Croquettes 55

Ricotta Stuffed Aubergine 56

Potato Hay 56

Butternut Squash 57

Cheesy Garlic Asparagus 57

Egg Fried Rice 57

Crispy Cinnamon French Toast 58

Tex Mex Hash Browns 58

Grilled Bacon And Cheese 59

Air Fryer Corn On The Cob 59

Celery Root Fries 60

Garlic And Parsley Potatoes 60

Crispy Sweet & Spicy Cauliflower 60

Sweet Potato Wedges

Servings:4

Cooking Time:20 Minutes

Ingredients:

- ½ tsp garlic powder
- ½ tsp cumin
- ½ tsp smoked paprika
- ½ tsp cayenne pepper
- ½ tsp salt
- ½ tsp black pepper
- 1 tsp dried chives
- 4 tbsp olive oil
- 3 large sweet potatoes, cut into wedges

Directions:

1. Preheat the air fryer to 180 °C / 350 °F and line the bottom of the basket with parchment paper.
2. In a bowl, mix the garlic powder, cumin, smoked paprika, cayenne pepper, salt, black pepper, and dried chives until combined.
3. Whisk in the olive oil and coat the sweet potato wedges in the spicy oil mixture.
4. Transfer the coated sweet potatoes to the air fryer and close the lid. Cook for 20 minutes until cooked and crispy. Serve hot as a side with your main meal.

Sweet Potato Tots

Servings: 24

Cooking Time:xx

Ingredients:

- 2 sweet potatoes, peeled
- ½ tsp cajun seasoning
- Olive oil cooking spray
- Sea salt to taste

Directions:

1. Boil the sweet potatoes in a pan for about 15 minutes, allow to cool
2. Grate the sweet potato and mix in the cajun seasoning
3. Form into tot shaped cylinders
4. Spray the air fryer with oil, place the tots in the air fryer
5. Sprinkle with salt and cook for 8 minutes at 200ºC, turn and cook for another 8 minutes

Ranch-style Potatoes

Servings: 2

Cooking Time:xx

Ingredients:

- 300g baby potatoes, washed
- 1 tbsp olive oil
- 3 tbsp dry ranch seasoning

Directions:

1. Preheat the air fryer to 220°C
2. Cut the potatoes in half
3. Take a mixing bowl and combine the olive oil with the ranch seasoning
4. Add the potatoes to the bowl and toss to coat
5. Cook for 15 minutes, shaking halfway through

Homemade Croquettes

Servings:4

Cooking Time:15 Minutes

Ingredients:

- 400 g / 14 oz white rice, uncooked
- 1 onion, sliced
- 2 cloves garlic, finely sliced
- 2 eggs, beaten
- 50 g / 3.5 oz parmesan cheese, grated
- 1 tsp salt
- 1 tsp black pepper
- 50 g / 3.5 oz breadcrumbs
- 1 tsp dried oregano

Directions:

1. In a large mixing bowl, combine the white rice, onion slices, garlic cloves slices, one beaten egg, parmesan cheese, and a sprinkle of salt and pepper.
2. Whisk the second egg in a separate bowl and place the breadcrumbs into another bowl.
3. Shape the mixture into 12 even croquettes and roll evenly in the egg, followed by the breadcrumbs.
4. Preheat the air fryer to 190 °C / 375 °F and line the bottom of the basket with parchment paper.
5. Place the croquettes in the lined air fryer basket and cook for 15 minutes, turning halfway through, until crispy and golden. Enjoy while hot as a side to your main dish.

Ricotta Stuffed Aubergine

Servings: 2

Cooking Time:xx

Ingredients:

- 1 aubergine
- 150g ricotta cheese
- 75g Parmesan cheese, plus an extra 75g for the breading
- 1 tsp garlic powder
- 3 tbsp parsley
- 1 egg, plus an extra 2 eggs for the breading
- 300g pork rind crumbs
- 2 tsp Italian seasoning

Directions:

1. Cut the aubergine into rounds, about 1/2" in thickness
2. Line a baking sheet with parchment and arrange the rounds on top, sprinkling with salt
3. Place another sheet of parchment on top and place something heavy on top to get rid of excess water
4. Leave for 30 minutes
5. Take a bowl and combine the egg, ricotta, 75g Parmesan and parsley, until smooth
6. Remove the parchment from the aubergine and wipe off the salt
7. Take a tablespoon of the ricotta mixture and place on top of each round of aubergine, spreading with a knife
8. Place in the freezer for a while to set
9. Take a bowl and add the two eggs, the pork rinds, parmesan and seasonings, and combine
10. Remove the aubergine from the freezer and coat each one in the mixture completely
11. Place back in the freezer for 45 minutes
12. Cook in the air fryer for 8 minutes at 250ºC

Potato Hay

Servings: 4

Cooking Time:xx

Ingredients:

- 2 potatoes
- 1 tbsp oil
- Salt and pepper to taste

Directions:

1. Cut the potatoes into spirals
2. Soak in a bowl of water for 20 minutes, drain and pat dry
3. Add oil, salt and pepper and mix well to coat
4. Preheat air fryer to 180ºC
5. Add potatoes to air fryer and cook for 5 minutes, toss then cook for another 12 until golden brown

Butternut Squash

Servings: 4

Cooking Time:xx

Ingredients:

- 500 g/1 lb. 2 oz. butternut squash, chopped into 2.5-cm/1-in. cubes
- 1 tablespoon olive oil or avocado oil
- 1 teaspoon smoked paprika
- 1 teaspoon dried oregano
- ½ teaspoon salt
- ¼ teaspoon freshly ground black pepper

Directions:

1. Preheat the air-fryer to 180ºC/350ºF.
2. In a bowl toss the butternut squash cubes in the oil and all the seasonings.
3. Add the butternut squash cubes to the preheated air-fryer and air-fry for 16–18 minutes, shaking the drawer once during cooking.

Cheesy Garlic Asparagus

Servings: 4

Cooking Time:xx

Ingredients:

- 1 tsp olive oil
- 500g asparagus
- 1 tsp garlic salt
- 1 tbsp grated parmesan cheese
- Salt and pepper for seasoning

Directions:

1. Preheat the air fryer to 270ºC
2. Clean the asparagus and cut off the bottom 1”
3. Pat dry and place in the air fryer, covering with the oil
4. Sprinkle the parmesan and garlic salt on top, seasoning to your liking
5. Cook for between 7 and 10 minutes
6. Add a little extra parmesan over the top before serving

Egg Fried Rice

Servings:2

Cooking Time:15 Minutes

Ingredients:

- 400 g / 14 oz cooked white or brown rice
- 100 g / 3.5 oz fresh peas and sweetcorn
- 2 tbsp olive oil
- 2 eggs, scrambled

Directions:

1. Preheat the air fryer to 150 °C / 300 °F and line the bottom of the basket with parchment paper.
2. In a bowl, mix the cooked white or brown rice and the fresh peas and sweetcorn.
3. Pour in 2 tbsp olive oil and toss to coat evenly. Stir in the scrambled eggs.
4. Transfer the egg rice into the lined air fryer basket, close the lid, and cook for 15 minutes until the eggs are cooked and the rice is soft.
5. Serve as a side dish with some cooked meat or tofu.

Crispy Cinnamon French Toast

Servings:2

Cooking Time:5 Minutes

Ingredients:

- 4 slices white bread
- 4 eggs
- 200 ml milk (cow's milk, cashew milk, soy milk, or oat milk)
- 2 tbsp granulated sugar
- 1 tsp brown sugar
- 1 tsp vanilla extract
- ½ tsp ground cinnamon

Directions:

1. Preheat your air fryer to 150 °C / 300 °F and line the bottom of the basket with parchment paper.
2. Cut each of the bread slices into 2 even rectangles and set them aside.
3. In a mixing bowl, whisk together the 4 eggs, milk, granulated sugar, brown sugar, vanilla extract, and ground cinnamon.
4. Soak the bread pieces in the egg mixture until they are fully covered and soaked in the mixture.
5. Place the coated bread slices in the lined air fryer, close the lid, and cook for 4-5 minutes until the bread is crispy and golden.
6. Serve the French toast slices with whatever toppings you desire.

Tex Mex Hash Browns

Servings: 4

Cooking Time:xx

Ingredients:

- 500g potatoes cut into cubes
- 1 tbsp olive oil
- 1 red pepper
- 1 onion
- 1 jalapeño pepper
- ½ tsp taco seasoning
- ½ tsp cumin
- Salt and pepper to taste

Directions:

1. Soak the potatoes in water for 20 minutes
2. Heat the air fryer to 160ºC
3. Drain the potatoes and coat with olive oil
4. Add to the air fryer and cook for 18 minutes
5. Mix the remaining ingredients in a bowl, add the potatoes and mix well
6. Place the mix into the air fryer cook for 6 minutes, shake and cook for a further 5 minutes

Grilled Bacon And Cheese

Servings: 2

Cooking Time:xx

Ingredients:

- 4 slices of regular bread
- 1 tbsp butter
- 2 slices cheddar cheese
- 5 slices bacon, pre-cooked
- 2 slices mozzarella cheese

Directions:

1. Place the butter into the microwave to melt
2. Spread the butter onto one side of the bread slices
3. Place one slice of bread into the fryer basket, with the buttered side facing downwards
4. Place the cheddar on top, followed by the bacon, mozzarella and the other slice of bread, with the buttered side facing upwards
5. Set your fryer to 170°C and cook the sandwich for 4 minutes
6. Turn the sandwich over and cook for another 3 minutes
7. Turn the sandwich out and serve whilst hot
8. Repeat with the other remaining sandwich

Air Fryer Corn On The Cob

Servings: 2

Cooking Time:xx

Ingredients:

- 2 corn on the cob
- 2 tbsp melted butter
- A pinch of salt
- 1/2 tsp dried parsley
- 2 tbsp grated parmesan

Directions:

1. Preheat the air fryer to 270°C
2. Take a bowl and combine the melted butter, salt and parsley
3. Brush the corn with the mixture
4. Add the corn inside the air fryer and cook for 14 minutes
5. Remove the corn from the fryer and roll in the grated cheese

Celery Root Fries

Servings: 2

Cooking Time:xx

Ingredients:

- ½ celeriac, cut into sticks
- 500ml water
- 1 tbsp lime juice
- 1 tbsp olive oil
- 75g mayo
- 1 tbsp mustard
- 1 tbsp powdered horseradish

Directions:

1. Put celeriac in a bowl, add water and lime juice, soak for 30 minutes
2. Preheat air fryer to 200
3. Mix together the mayo, horseradish powder and mustard, refrigerate
4. Drain the celeriac, drizzle with oil and season with salt and pepper
5. Place in the air fryer and cook for about 10 minutes turning halfway
6. Serve with the mayo mix as a dip

Garlic And Parsley Potatoes

Servings: 4

Cooking Time:xx

Ingredients:

- 500g baby potatoes, cut into quarters
- 1 tbsp oil
- 1 tsp salt
- ½ tsp garlic powder
- ½ tsp dried parsley

Directions:

1. Preheat air fryer to 175ºC
2. Combine potatoes and oil in a bowl
3. Add remaining ingredients and mix
4. Add to the air fryer and cook for about 25 minutes until golden brown, turning halfway through

Crispy Sweet & Spicy Cauliflower

Servings: 2

Cooking Time:xx

Ingredients:

- ½ a head of cauliflower
- 1 teaspoon sriracha sauce
- 1 teaspoon soy sauce (or tamari)
- ½ teaspoon maple syrup
- 2 teaspoons olive oil or avocado oil

Directions:

1. Preheat the air-fryer to 180ºC/350ºF.
2. Chop the cauliflower into florets with a head size of roughly 5 cm/1 in. Place the other ingredients in a bowl and mix together, then add the florets and toss to coat them.
3. Add the cauliflower to the preheated air-fryer and air-fry for 12 minutes, shaking the drawer a couple of times during cooking.

Desserts Recipes

Chocolate Orange Fondant 62

Key Lime Cupcakes 62

New York Cheesecake 63

Chocolate-glazed Banana Slices 63

Apple Chips With Yogurt Dip 64

Pumpkin Spiced Bread Pudding 64

Profiteroles 65

Banana Maple Flapjack 65

Strawberry Danish 66

Apple And Cinnamon Empanadas 66

Lava Cakes 67

Blueberry Muffins 67

Chonut Holes 68

Lemon Pies 68

Chocolate Orange Fondant

Servings: 4

Cooking Time:xx

Ingredients:

- 2 tbsp self raising flour
- 4 tbsp caster sugar
- 115g dark chocolate
- 115g butter
- 1 medium orange rind and juice
- 2 eggs

Directions:

1. Preheat the air fryer to 180ºC and grease 4 ramekins
2. Place the chocolate and butter in a glass dish and melt over a pan of hot water, stir until the texture is creamy
3. Beat the eggs and sugar together until pale and fluffy
4. Add the orange and egg mix to the chocolate and mix
5. Stir in the flour until fully mixed together
6. Put the mix into the ramekins, place in the air fryer and cook for 12 minutes. Leave to stand for 2 minutes before serving

Key Lime Cupcakes

Servings: 6

Cooking Time:xx

Ingredients:

- 250g Greek yogurt
- 200g soft cheese
- 2 eggs
- Juice and rind of 2 limes
- 1 egg yolk
- ¼ cup caster sugar
- 1 tsp vanilla essence

Directions:

1. Mix the Greek yogurt and soft cheese together until smooth
2. Add the eggs and mix, add the lime juice, rind, vanilla and caster sugar and mix well
3. Fill 6 cupcake cases with the mix and place the rest to one side
4. Place in the air fryer and cook at 160ºC for 10 minutes then another 10 minutes at 180ºC
5. Place the remaining mix into a piping bag, once the cupcakes have cooled pipe on the top and place in the fridge to set

New York Cheesecake

Servings: 8

Cooking Time:xx

Ingredients:

- 225g plain flour
- 100g brown sugar
- 100g butter
- 50g melted butter
- 1 tbsp vanilla essence
- 750g soft cheese
- 2 cups caster sugar
- 3 large eggs
- 50ml quark

Directions:

1. Add the flour, sugar, and 100g butter to a bowl and mix until combined. Form into biscuit shapes place in the air fryer and cook for 15 minutes at 180ºC
2. Grease a springform tin
3. Break the biscuits up and mix with the melted butter, press firmly into the tin
4. Mix the soft cheese and sugar in a bowl until creamy, add the eggs and vanilla and mix. Mix in the quark
5. Pour the cheesecake batter into the pan
6. Place in your air fryer and cook for 30 minutes at 180ºC. Leave in the air fryer for 30 minutes whilst it cools
7. Refrigerate for 6 hours

Chocolate-glazed Banana Slices

Servings:2

Cooking Time:10 Minutes

Ingredients:

- 2 bananas
- 1 tbsp honey
- 1 tbsp chocolate spread, melted
- 2 tbsp milk chocolate chips

Directions:

1. Preheat the air fryer to 180 °C / 350 °F. Remove the mesh basket from the machine and line it with parchment paper.
2. Cut the two bananas into even slices and place them in the lined air fryer basket.
3. In a small bowl, mix the honey and melted chocolate spread. Use a brush to glaze the banana slices. Carefully press the milk chocolate chips into the banana slices enough so that they won't fall out when you transfer the bananas into the air fryer.
4. Carefully slide the mesh basket into the air fryer, close the lid, and cook for 10 minutes until the bananas are hot and the choc chips have melted.
5. Enjoy the banana slices on their own or with a side of ice cream.

Apple Chips With Yogurt Dip

Servings: 4

Cooking Time:xx

Ingredients:

- 1 apple
- 1 tsp cinnamon
- 2 tsp oil
- Cooking spray
- 25g greek yogurt
- 1 tbsp almond butter
- 1 tsp honey

Directions:

1. Thinly slice the apple, place in a bowl and coat with cinnamon and oil
2. Coat the air fryer with cooking spray and add the apple slices
3. Cook the slices for 12 minutes at 180ºC
4. Mix the butter, honey and yogurt together and serve with the apple slices as a dip

Pumpkin Spiced Bread Pudding

Servings: 2

Cooking Time:xx

Ingredients:

- 175g heavy cream
- 500g pumpkin puree
- 30ml milk
- 25g sugar
- 1 large egg, plus one extra yolk
- ⅛ tsp salt
- ½ tsp pumpkin spice
- 500g cubed crusty bread
- 4 tbsp butter

Directions:

1. Place all of the ingredients apart from the bread and butter into a bowl and mix.
2. Add the bread and melted butter to the bowl and mix well
3. Heat the air fryer to 175ºC
4. Pour the mix into a baking tin and cook in the air fryer for 35-40 minutes
5. Serve with maple cream

Profiteroles

Servings: 9

Cooking Time:xx

Ingredients:

- 100g butter
- 200g plain flour
- 6 eggs
- 300ml water
- 2 tsp vanilla extract
- 300ml whipped cream
- 100g milk chocolate
- 2 tbsp whipped cream
- 50g butter
- 2 tsp icing sugar

Directions:

1. Preheat the air fryer to 170°C
2. Place the butter and water in a pan over a medium heat, bring to the boil, remove from the heat and stir in the flour
3. Return to the heat stirring until a dough is formed
4. Mix in the eggs and stir until mixture is smooth, make into profiterole shapes and cook in the air fryer for 10 minutes
5. For the filling whisk together 300ml whipped cream, vanilla extract and the icing sugar
6. For the topping place the butter, 2tbsp whipped cream and chocolate in a bowl and melt over a pan of hot water until mixed together
7. Pipe the filling into the roles and finish off with a chocolate topping

Banana Maple Flapjack

Servings:9

Cooking Time:xx

Ingredients:

- 100 g/7 tablespoons butter (or plant-based spread if you wish)
- 75 g/5 tablespoons maple syrup
- 2 ripe bananas, mashed well with the back of a fork
- 1 teaspoon vanilla extract
- 240 g/2½ cups rolled oats/quick-cooking oats

Directions:

1. Gently heat the butter and maple syrup in a medium saucepan over a low heat until melted. Stir in the mashed banana, vanilla and oats and combine all ingredients. Pour the flapjack mixture into a 15 x 15-cm/6 x 6-in. baking pan and cover with foil.
2. Preheat the air-fryer to 200°C/400°F.
3. Add the baking pan to the preheated air-fryer and air-fry for 12 minutes, then remove the foil and cook for a further 4 minutes to brown the top. Leave to cool before cutting into 9 squares.

Strawberry Danish

Servings: 2

Cooking Time:xx

Ingredients:

- 1 tube crescent roll dough
- 200g cream cheese
- 25g strawberry jam
- 50g diced strawberries
- 225g powdered sugar
- 2-3 tbsp cream

Directions:

1. Roll out the dough
2. Spread the cream cheese over the dough, cover in jam
3. Sprinkle with strawberries
4. Roll the dough up from the short side and pinch to seal
5. Line the air fryer with parchment paper and spray with cooking spray
6. Place the dough in the air fryer and cook at 175ºC for 20 minutes
7. Mix the cream with the powdered sugar and drizzle on top once cooked

Apple And Cinnamon Empanadas

Servings: 12

Cooking Time:xx

Ingredients:

- 12 empanada wraps
- 2 diced apples
- 2 tbsp honey
- 1 tsp vanilla extract
- 1 tsp cinnamon
- ⅛ tsp nutmeg
- Olive oil spray
- 2 tsp cornstarch
- 1 tsp water

Directions:

1. Place apples, cinnamon, honey, vanilla and nutmeg in a pan cook for 2-3 minutes until apples are soft
2. Mix the cornstarch and water add to the pan and cook for 30 seconds
3. Add the apple mix to each of the empanada wraps
4. Roll the wrap in half, pinch along the edges, fold the edges in then continue to roll to seal
5. Place in the air fryer and cook at 200ºC for 8 minutes, turn and cook for another 10 minutes

Lava Cakes

Servings: 4

Cooking Time:xx

Ingredients:

- 1 ½ tbsp self raising flour
- 3 ½ tbsp sugar
- 150g butter
- 150g dark chocolate, chopped
- 2 eggs

Directions:

1. Preheat the air fryer to 175°C
2. Grease 4 ramekin dishes
3. Melt chocolate and butter in the microwave for about 3 minutes
4. Whisk the eggs and sugar together until pale and frothy
5. Pour melted chocolate into the eggs and stir in the flour
6. Fill the ramekins ¾ full, place in the air fryer and cook for 10 minutes

Blueberry Muffins

Servings: 12

Cooking Time:xx

Ingredients:

- 500g cups self raising flour
- 50g monk fruit
- 50g cream
- 225g oil
- 2 eggs
- 200g blueberries
- Zest and juice of 1 lemon
- 1 tbsp vanilla

Directions:

1. Mix together flour and sugar, set aside
2. In another bowl mix the remaining ingredients
3. Mix in the flour
4. Spoon the mix into silicone cupcake cases
5. Place in the air fryer and cook at 160°C for about 10 minutes

Chonut Holes

Servings: 12

Cooking Time:xx

Ingredients:

- 225g flour
- 75g sugar
- 1 tsp baking powder
- ¼ tsp cinnamon
- 2 tbsp sugar
- ½ tsp salt
- 2 tbsp aquafaba
- 1 tbsp melted coconut oil
- 75ml soy milk
- 2 tsp cinnamon

Directions:

1. In a bowl mix the flour, ¼ cup sugar, baking powder, ¼ tsp cinnamon and salt
2. Add the aquafaba, coconut oil and soy milk mix well
3. In another bowl mix 2 tsp cinnamon and 2 tbsp sugar
4. Line the air fryer with parchment paper
5. Divide the dough into 12 pieces and dredge with the cinnamon sugar mix
6. Place in the air fryer at 185°C and cook for 6-8 minutes, don't shake them

Lemon Pies

Servings: 6

Cooking Time:xx

Ingredients:

- 1 pack of pastry
- 1 egg beaten
- 200g lemon curd
- 225g powdered sugar
- ½ lemon

Directions:

1. Preheat the air fryer to 180°C
2. Cut out 6 circles from the pastry using a cookie cutter
3. Add 1 tbsp of lemon curd to each circle, brush the edges with egg and fold over
4. Press around the edges of the dough with a fork to seal
5. Brush the pies with the egg and cook in the air fryer for 10 minutes
6. Mix the lemon juice with the powdered sugar to make the icing and drizzle on the cooked pies

Measurement Conversions

BASIC KITCHEN CONVERSIONS & EQUIVALENT

DRY MEASUREMENTS CONVERSION CHART

3 TEASPOONS = 1 TABLESPOON = 1/16 CUP

6 TEASPOONS = 2 TABLESPOONS = 1/8 CUP

12 TEASPOONS = 4 TABLESPOONS = 1/4 CUP

24 TEASPOONS = 8 TABLESPOONS = 1/2 CUP

36 TEASPOONS = 12 TABLESPOONS = 3/4 CUP

48 TEASPOONS = 16 TABLESPOONS = 1 CUP

METRIC TO US COOKING CONVER SIONS

OVEN TEMPERATURE

120℃ = 250° F

160℃ = 320° F

180℃ = 350° F

205℃ = 400° F

220℃ = 425° F

OVEN TEMPERATURE

8 FLUID OUNCES = 1 CUP = 1/2 PINT = 1/4 QUART

16 FLUID OUNCES = 2 CUPS = 1 PINT = 1/2 QUART

32 FLUID OUNCES = 4 CUPS = 2 PINTS = 1 QUART

= 1/4 GALLON

128 FLUID OUNCES = 16 CUPS = 8 PINTS = 4 QUARTS = 1 GALLON

BAKING IN GRAMS

1 CUP FLOUR = 140 GRAMS

1 CUP SUGAR = 150 GRAMS

1 CUP POWDERED SUGAR = 160 GRAMS

1 CUP HEAVY CREAM = 235 GRAMS

VOLUME

1 MILLILITER = 1/5 TEASPOON

5 ML = 1 TEASPOON

15 ML = 1 TABLESPOON

240 ML = 1 CUP OR 8 FLUID OUNCES

1 LITER = 34 FL. OUNCES

WEIGHT

1 GRAM = .035 OUNCES

100 GRAMS = 3.5 OUNCES

500 GRAMS = 1.1 POUNDS

1 KILOGRAM = 35 OUNCES

US TO METRIC COOKING CONVERSIONS

1/5 TSP = 1 ML

1 TSP = 5 ML

1 TBSP = 15 ML

1 FL OUNCE = 30 ML

1 CUP = 237 ML

1 PINT (2 CUPS) = 473 ML

1 QUART (4 CUPS) = .95 LITER

1 GALLON (16 CUPS) = 3.8 LITERS

1 OZ = 28 GRAMS

1 POUND = 454 GRAMS

BUTTER

1 CUP BUTTER = 2 STICKS = 8 OUNCES = 230 GRAMS = 8 TABLESPOONS

BUTTER

1 CUP = 8 FLUID OUNCES

1 CUP = 16 TABLESPOONS

1 CUP = 48 TEASPOONS

1 CUP = 1/2 PINT

1 CUP = 1/4 QUART

1 CUP = 1/16 GALLON

1 CUP = 240 ML

BAKING PAN CONVERSIONS

1 CUP ALL-PURPOSE FLOUR = 4.5 OZ

1 CUP ROLLED OATS = 3 OZ 1 LARGE EGG = 1.7 OZ

1 CUP BUTTER = 8 OZ

1 CUP MILK = 8 OZ

1 CUP HEAVY CREAM = 8.4 OZ

1 CUP GRANULATED SUGAR = 7.1 OZ

1 CUP PACKED BROWN SUGAR = 7.75 OZ

1 CUP VEGETABLE OIL = 7.7 OZ

1 CUP UNSIFTED POWDERED SUGAR = 4.4 OZ

BAKING PAN CONVERSIONS

9-INCH ROUND CAKE PAN = 12 CUPS

10-INCH TUBE PAN =16 CUPS

11-INCH BUNDT PAN = 12 CUPS

9-INCH SPRINGFORM PAN = 10 CUPS

9 X 5 INCH LOAF PAN = 8 CUPS

9-INCH SQUARE PAN = 8 CUPS

Recipe ....

From the kicthen of ....

Serves .... Prep time .... Cook time ....

☐ Difficulty ☐ Easy ☐ Medium ☐ Hard

Ingredient

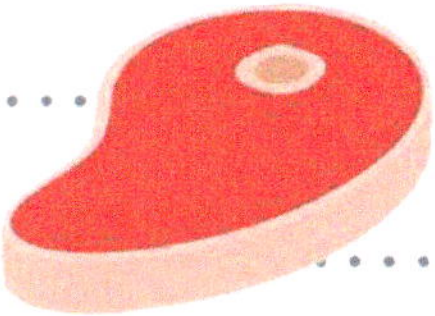

Directions

Recipe ....

From the kicthen of ....

Serves .... Prep time .... Cook time ....

☐ Difficulty ☐ Easy ☐ Medium ☐ Hard

Ingredient

Directions

Appendix : Recipes Index

A

Air-fried Pickles 17
Air Fryer Cheese Sandwich 22
Air Fryer Sesame Chicken Thighs 33
Air Fryer Tuna 50
Air Fryer Corn On The Cob 59
Apple Chips With Yogurt Dip 64
Apple And Cinnamon Empanadas 66

B

Bocconcini Balls 8
Breakfast Sausage Burgers 11
Baked Aubergine Slices With Yogurt Dressing 24
Buffalo Chicken Wontons 31
Buttermilk Chicken 32
Bacon Wrapped Chicken Thighs 36
Buttermilk Pork Chops 38
Beef Satay 44
Butter Steak & Asparagus 44
Beer Battered Fish Tacos 48
Baked Panko Cod 49
Butternut Squash 57
Banana Maple Flapjack 65
Blueberry Muffins 67

C

Courgette Fries 12
Cheesy Sausage Breakfast Pockets 13
Corn Nuts 15
Cheese Wontons 20
Camembert & Soldiers 26
Crispy Cornish Hen 30
Cheddar & Bbq Stuffed Chicken 32
Chicken Kiev 34
Chicken & Potatoes 35
Chicken And Wheat Stir Fry 36
Crunchy Fish 46
Chilli Lime Tilapia 49
Cheesy Garlic Asparagus 57
Crispy Cinnamon French Toast 58
Celery Root Fries 60
Crispy Sweet & Spicy Cauliflower 60
Chocolate Orange Fondant 62
Chocolate-glazed Banana Slices 63
Chonut Holes 68

E

European Pancakes 10
Egg Fried Rice 57

F

French Toast 10
Flat Mushroom Pizzas 28
Fish In Foil 51
Fish Sticks With Tartar Sauce Batter 52

G

Garlic Parmesan Fried Chicken Wings 35
Grilled Bacon And Cheese 59
Garlic And Parsley Potatoes 60

H

Hawaiian Chicken 34
Homemade Crispy Pepperoni Pizza 39
Homemade Croquettes 55

J

Jamaican Jerk Pork 41

K

Korean Chicken Wings 19
Key Lime Cupcakes 62

L

Loaded Hash Browns 11
Lamb Burgers 39
Lobster Tails 50

Lava Cakes 67
Lemon Pies 68

M

Monte Cristo Breakfast Sandwich 8
Meaty Egg Cups 12
Mac & Cheese Bites 18
Mushroom Pasta 25

N

New York Cheesecake 63

O

Onion Pakoda 20

P

Polenta Fries 9
Pasta Chips 16
Pork Jerky 16
Potato Gratin 23
Pork Chilli Cheese Dogs 38
Pork Taquitos 42
Pork Chops With Raspberry And Balsamic 43
Peppery Lemon Shrimp 47
Potato Hay 56
Pumpkin Spiced Bread Pudding 64
Profiteroles 65

R

Roasted Almonds 18
Roast Cauliflower & Broccoli 25
Roasted Cauliflower 27
Ranch Style Fish Fillets 51
Ranch-style Potatoes 55
Ricotta Stuffed Aubergine 56

S

Sweet Potato Fries 9
Spicy Chickpeas 17
Salt And Vinegar Chickpeas 18
Spicy Peanuts 19
Stuffed Peppers 23
Spinach And Egg Air Fryer Breakfast Muffins 28
Spicy Chicken Wing Drummettes 33
Salt And Pepper Belly Pork 40
Steak Dinner 42
Shrimp With Yum Yum Sauce 46
Salt & Pepper Calamari 48
Sweet Potato Tots 54
Sweet Potato Wedges 54
Strawberry Danish 66

T

Tangy Breakfast Hash 13
Thai Bites 15
Tempura Veggies 22
Tomato And Herb Tofu 26
Two-step Pizza 27
Turkey Cutlets In Mushroom Sauce 30
Turkey And Mushroom Burgers 31
Traditional Empanadas 41
Tahini Beef Bites 43
Thai Fish Cakes 47
Traditional Fish And Chips 50
Thai Salmon Patties 51
Traditional Fish And Chips 52
Tex Mex Hash Browns 58

V

Veggie Bakes 24
Vegetable & Beef Frittata 40

Printed in Great Britain
by Amazon

30887207R00044